The Roller Coaster Inside

The Roller Coaster Inside

Life In Limbo

K.BROOKS

authorHOUSE®

AuthorHouse™ UK
1663 Liberty Drive
Bloomington, IN 47403 USA
www.authorhouse.co.uk
Phone: 0800.197.4150

Published by AuthorHouse 05/18/2015

ISBN: 978-1-5049-4282-9 (sc)
ISBN: 978-1-5049-4283-6 (e)

Print information available on the last page.

*Any people depicted in stock imagery provided by Thinkstock are models,
and such images are being used for illustrative purposes only.
Certain stock imagery © Thinkstock.*

This book is printed on acid-free paper.

Contents

Prologue

Throughout the book, you will experience the highs and lows of what life throws at us and has thrown at me. Deep and sincere, each poem has been written to express the overwhelming feelings I have been subjected too and what a lot of you will have also felt. Each poem aims to reach out to the inner emotions we carry in order to connect with you- to let you know you are not alone with the burdens and the joys of life.

My background

A daughter to military parents I have never had a place I can really call home. With my mother being an RAF communications engineer and my father being an RAF policeman, life for me was never straight forward. From the age of eleven, I was subjected to my childhood and teenage years in boarding school where I felt confined, alone and helpless. I never really got along with any of my school mates unable to fit in and ride through school happily. I was shy and reserved for the first 4 years so, learning about the world and feeling trapped, I turned to poetry as a way to express how I was really feeling inside without being judged. It was an escape from reality. I met my best friend in the last two years of school whom I shared a room with. She filled me with hope and directed me through my dark stages, helping me battle the demons I was struggling with. I owe a lot of my success to her as she gave me the willpower and strength to make the most of my life. I am now at university studying animal behaviour and training, a part time event singer, part time delivery driver and a poet. Life is not easy and it will never run smoothly but being able to cope with the toughest bits helps me achieve the goals I want to.

Mother Nature

Global warming fills the earth,
The blanket of gas that we drown in,
Still we cannot resist the greed,
Temptation to want, not need.

The dark grey clouds that block the sun,
Hold thunder, lightning and the rain that's begun.
The battle that shall go on ahead,
Will leave thousands homeless and hundreds dead!

Mother nature, what have we done?
We kill your world, it's not for fun.
Look at the famine and look at the thirst,
Look at the men that destroy this earth!

Children run from their parents' death,
Not knowing the diseases that lie ahead.
Malaria will catch and kill their minds,
They'll cry and starve, get left behind.

I knew a man who went to war,
I saw his children scared, unsure,
The gas was slowly creeping in,
He choked and died and let it win.

Mother nature, what have we done?
We kill your world, it's not for fun.
Look at the famine and look at the thirst,
Look at us- we destroy our earth.

Northern lights

The glowing lights dance through the sky,
The outstanding rainbow reflects my eye,
The night so still, the ground so bare.
Yet the beauty of nature's heart lies there
Like a pulsing beat, the flash of green,
Then orange, then red, then aquamarine!
Like a bursting firework fires through the air,
Yet it paints a picture of a beauty so rare.
They shall call it the Northern lights,
The colour of the sky, the beauty of nights.

The spirit

This house tells a story of a girl who was ill,
Of how she died slowly, of how she was killed.
This grave holds a secret, of a bell that was placed,
In her coffin in hopes that she would soon wake.
But when the dawn broke, that bell would call,
Her mother would find it, but too late for the girl.
They opened her coffin, and there inside,
Laid the girl frozen screaming, with blood up the sides.
The spirit that wanders and haunts this place,
The one in the mirror, of poor Mary's face.

These moments

Moments last forever, and feelings can be strong,
But choices can be hard, and some can lead you on.
But once you've found your path, and battled your way through,
Some things they last forever, and those they can be true.

When you start, it's way below,
Your heart is hard and times are slow.
But when you move and get to see and touch and hear,
Just you and me.

You feel like you can't touch the ground,
Your eyes are blind, you hear no sound,
A feeling of floating, as light as air,
No worries, no stress, no panic, no care.

Lines have broken for dreams and reality,
It falls as one, everything's normality,
I hope this feeling lasts forever…
and if not, these moments I'll treasure.

The Orphan

I remember the good times, the fun we had
With my family- mum and dad.
I remember how we used to laugh,
That time was precious, but now is passed.

I saw the men crash through the door,
The way they thrust me to the floor,
Then they screamed and spat at me,
To get up and leave my family.

They split us up and took our names,
They gave us numbers, made us slaves.
The useless were stripped, taken away,
I knew where they went, it hurts to say.

I still hear deathly cries, people choking,
They would slowly die.
I knew my parents were not alive,
I am the orphan, the one that survived.

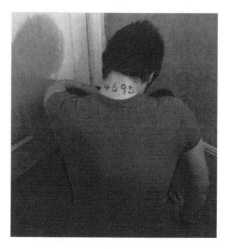

An anonymous love

How your eyes glisten in the sunlight,
How your breath makes me shiver,
When you're near my chest feels tight,
Whatever I look for, you deliver.
You have a presence that takes my breath away,
You give me butterflies of love,
There are a million things about you I could say,
But even with all the trees in the world,
That is still not enough.

Predator

I cannot run, I cannot hide,
From the thoughts that suffocate me,
Of what the world is really like,
From what we fail to see.

At the chime of night,
The predators come alive,
Doing the devils work,
The evil sure to thrive.

Oblivious to every vandal,
Blind to every thief,
Ignoring every kidnap,
Building on our grief.

Every murder shows,
How vulnerable we can be
Just living every day
We're never truly free.

Broken

Do you really care?
Do you know I hurt?
The memories that surround me,
The ones I can't convert.

They're the ones that haunt me,
Of when I was so young,
When I felt your arms around me,
My life not even begun.

But you emptied your embrace,
You took away my heart,
And now the hole is open,
From where you tore my chest apart.

This empty space kept growing,
And still you never knew,
The damage it was causing,
All you thought about was you.

The years just kept on going,
The wound still open wide,
The hurt forever growing,
For you're not at my side.

The adult shell I'm showing,
Of what I have to be,
Hides the little girl,
Of who she'll always be.

Face in the windowpane

Sanity has gone away
Time has come to stop
Reality is freezing over
All feelings not forgot

You popped up out of nowhere
And somehow took me over
Now you're done, now you're gone
But still there's yet no closure

The glass has frosted over
From where we once last stood
My breath is getting colder
My pain in tears have flood

The floor on which I'm breaking
My heads become insane
From memories of your face
In the windowpane.

The cycling motion

Confusion not the word
Timing is the worst
Feeling overwhelmed
My head about to burst

What must I do?
To keep the world at peace
My feelings at the bottom
Opinions become deceased

Trapped in cycling motion
My emotion needs control
Feelings are uncertain
My conscience needs parole

My dreams are my escape
To please none but me
Unfortunately my reality
Will never set me free.

The Space

Taken all for granted,
Of what we had before,
When we shared our home,
Best friends we were for sure.

Time was running out,
The sand was draining fast,
Memories flowing smoothly,
Down the minute hour glass.

We are moving forward,
In a changing time,
Of ever growing lives,
And you I've left behind.

Never looking back,
I carried on my way,
The space that comes between us,
Seems further every day.

My heart has felt the weather,
Of every storm there's been,
And nothing could prepare me,
For what was not foreseen.

The realisation made me mad,
The truth could not be hidden,
Of what I felt for you,
A love that is forbidden.

The rules denied me access,
To what I learnt too late,
My heart should be with you,
And shouldn't be with fate.

I'm sure you've often wondered,
If we could be more,
But my distractions hindered,
The feelings from your core.

Rushing realisation,
And learning things too late,
Made you run a mile,
And shut the friendship gate.

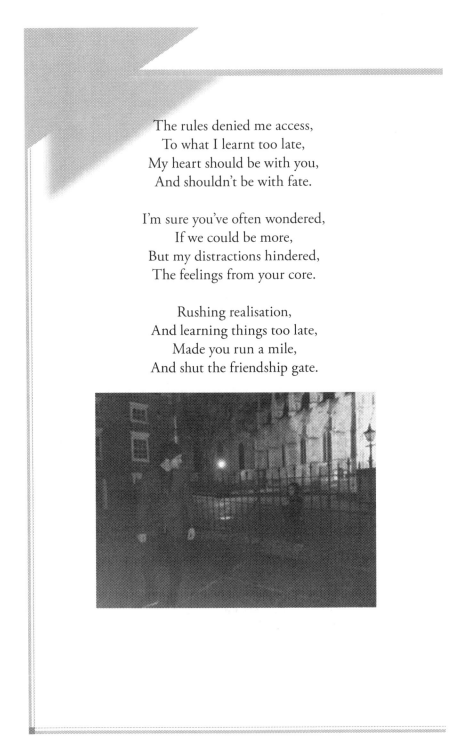

Taking over me

Feeling useless is not a dream,
This feeling lasts a light year,
For all my life lived without purpose,
Forever stuck in first gear.

A few rounds of cemented rotten luck,
Without a leg to stand on,
The nightmare continues on with me,
It won't be long before I'm gone.

Too much pain, too much hurt,
Washing over me,
Fills my lungs so I can't breathe,
Taking over me!

Will you see what I've become?
Without you be there to guide me,
Throughout my life left on my own,
Of what I'm left to be?

The little face behind the bars,
The girl you trapped inside,
The prison cell with tortured thoughts,
The ones she tries to hide.

She tries to change the way she looks,
To somehow set her free,
But this just covers up the truth,
Of what lies beneath.

Say what you'd do for me,
And tell me that you want me,
Love me like a mother should,
Please be there for me!

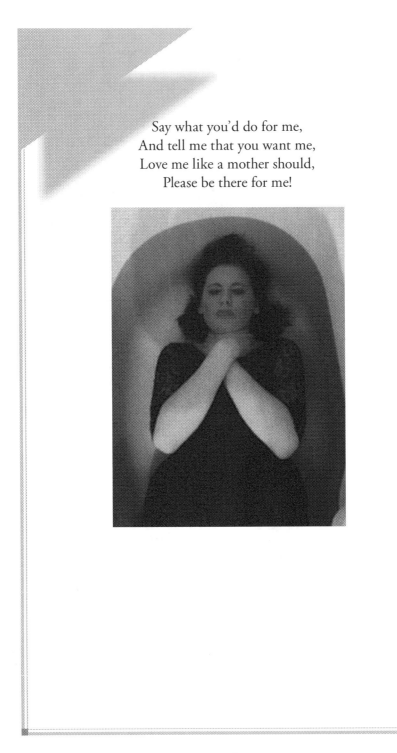

14

A soldier to my pain

The cycle keeps on going,
Around and around again,
The final phase the same each time,
The change keeps asking, "when"?

When do feelings grow?
Instead of fading out?
When does commitment excite?
Rather than hanging doubt?

Is nothing ever simple?
Does nothing ever change?
When will I become,
A soldier to my pain?

Battling with my thoughts,
Culling all my fear,
Laying the past to rest,
Helping my mind to clear.

When will I find the key?
To unlock the prison,
To unchain the girl inside,
To hold the heart she's given.

For the one she's waited,
To come and set her free,
One day I hope he comes,
I hope he rescues me.

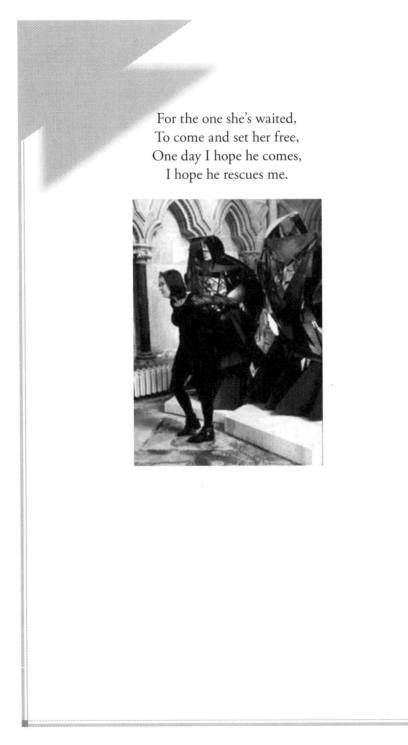

Disbelief in fairy tales

Can you feel my heart?
Can you see the vibe?
The one that glows between us,
That we don't need to hide.

The disbelief of what I've found,
Is only found in dreams,
Or seen in other people,
And fairy tales it seems.

This feeling resonates in me,
Deep inside my chest,
Pulsing through my veins,
My body cannot rest.

I see meadows in your eyes,
Affection in your mind,
Perfection on your lips,
A face that's so defined.

Through the passing time,
Of what we've grown to know,
The stories we have shared,
Affection we have shown.

First meeting still to come,
But from how you seem to be,
In you I keep on seeing,
A little piece of me.

Nothing's ever foolproof,
And walls will block our way,
The surrounding ring of fire,
Will find a price to pay.

Whatever be the obstacle,
Whatever be the doubt,
Any time you worry,
Will always be worked out.

I will go the distance,
I will make the time,
I'll display all my feelings,
To let you know you're mine.

I'll ponder our adventure,
Of what there is to come,
My thoughts I write to you,
We'll never come undone.

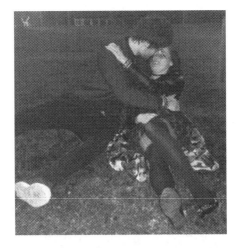

Eye of the storm

Caught up in the hurricane,
Trapped in the eye of the storm,
The whirlwind started off so slow,
But now my strength has worn.

Building pressures underneath,
What I face alone,
Adding all your pain on me,
Has my balanced scales all blown.

Tug of war is what it is,
The rope burn slices through,
The toughened skin I'm seen to wear,
They haven't got a clue.

Of all the burden I am hiding,
Of all the built up hate,
Of what my life has thrown at me,
Sees the persona I create.

After all I'm only human,
I can only take so much,
And when I say I've had enough,
Please don't hold a grudge.

I will still do overtime,
And help you with your issues,
But I'm still only just a girl,
So your battles I may lose.

Daffodils

The whispering wind that sways the grass,
A sign that freezing winter's passed,
When shoots pop up to meet the sun,
It's the sign that spring's at last begun.
The golden bud that stands so tall,
Sparkles with dew, outshines them all,
And when it opens, it will glow,
The wind will whisper you're beautiful.

I remember

I remember, the time we used to spend together.
I remember, lying under the stars and only hearing your heart beat.
I remember, looking into your eyes and
knowing I could always trust you.
I remember, the way you used to hold me and
tell me everything would be ok.
I remember, you telling me not to worry about you
and that you would return to my arms soon.
I remember, the last letter I received from you.
I remember.

Passion

When you feel lost and tired,
And you can't sleep,
When your body is numb,
Your thoughts so deep.

When your eyes are dazed,
And you feel so weak,
The whole world matters,
Yet you can't speak.

This time is taken to reflect,
On past disasters you least expect,
And time again you feel let down,
You're told more chances will come around.

But the way I am,
And the way I feel,
Is so intense,
Becomes surreal.

And now I know,
It will take the one,
To read me through,
And hold me strong.

Because I'm different,
My passion great,
My grip is tight,
It's down to fate.

I'm just a girl

I'm just a girl, no need to love me
I'm only human, no need to haunt me
I'm only 20, no need to cradle me
I'm forever lost, no need to guide me.

You're just a lullaby, singing in my head
You're just a nightmare, left my childhood dead
You're just a memory, living in my mind
You're just a piece, my life has left behind

They don't know, the story I hold
They don't know, the promise I was told
They don't know, the scars inside me
They don't know, the horrors I see.

We're only bound by blood
We're just a shell once stood
We're a page in a history book
Our future is only what you took.

Scars

My mind is numb,
My hands are weak,
My eyes are stung,
My lips can't speak.

My tears that fall,
My thoughts of you,
I feel so small,
Like nothing's true.

My legs they shake,
My stomach churns,
Was all this fake?
And all I've learned.

You felt so real,
We looked so right,
But how you feel,
I've lost this fight.

What I know,
I can't escape,
My heart controls,
So I can't concentrate.

So I must write,
To keep me sane,
I feel so light,
My body in pain.

This is what you make me see,
This is what you've done to me.

The hands of time

Turn back the clock,
Lock your demons away,
All is not forgot,
The part you did play.

What did you see?
When I was so young,
What did you have planned?
Before I'd even begun.

Did you see yourself dead?
In the mind I have now,
Could you have imagined?
How you'd let me drown.

If I could freeze time,
I'd have you right here,
I wouldn't be speaking,
To your grave through my tears.

Turn back the clock,
Lock your demons away,
All not is forgot,
The part you did play.

Open eyes

For a while I saw you
When we were just children
But our differences made us blind
And left our soul mates far behind.
We carried on with our years,
Not thinking much- just our fears,
And we grew up strong and kind,
Learning, searching, new things to find,
Feeling friendly, we both would know,
Our different sides had changed us so,
And as of that we began to speak,
Every day of every week,
Now attached we can't let go,
What's to come?
What's left to know?
But here we are,
Our feelings grown,
No longer will I be alone,
Time is endless, distance great,
But this is nothing and it is fate.

Magnets

Possessing all my actions,
Claiming all my thoughts,
Controlling all my feelings,
Not caring if I'm caught.

Burning bright with passion,
in just a second of bliss,
the earth can fade away,
from purely just your kiss.
The static feeling from your touch,
The shivers through my spine,
That ice cold feeling through my body,
not aware of the loss of time.

And boy you make me crazy,
My logic fades to black,
And I try hard to stay away,
But your magnets pull me back.

You run your fingers through my hair,
You hold me close and strong,
But this just makes me want you more,
Although I know it's wrong.

But all control I lose,
When I'm in your embrace,
When your lips touch mine,
And when I see your face.

This feeling lasts for minutes,
your effect can last for days,
my memory holds you strong,
But my dreams are just a haze.

My want for you has made me mad,
your scent just like a drug,
I crave to see you every day,
I get my fix from just your hug.

And when I see you next,
I'll want my fix again,
But you will turn around and say,
I'm sorry you're just a friend.

Yo-Yo

So now you're back again,
You want to know me now,
You say it's not pretend,
Although you've let me down.

So when I'm taken,
You want me back,
Seeing envy in your eyes,
And yes- this is a fact.

But when I'm open,
I'm brushed aside,
You couldn't care less,
So you run and hide.

You play me like a yo-yo,
You spin me up and down,
And I have played your silly games,
But my sense has come around.

Even though I want you badly,
I have learnt to see,
Through your lies, and in your mind,
That you're no good for me.

These words are just a token

You are the light in me,
You mean the world I see,
Even when we're apart,
You are the burning in my heart.

You are the gold hidden in the mine,
You're in my dreams, and in my mind,
You are the objects I touch and see,
You are the person to always find me.

You've made me blind from love so raw,
That just makes me want you more,
You've stolen my heart and sewn it to yours,
So when it is snagged, you'll patch up the sores.

Wherever I go you'll always be near,
Whatever I do I won't have to fear,
And when I cry I know I'll stop,
Because I'm remembered and not forgot.

My love for you will never fade,
Our sewn up heart cannot be frayed,
We are one that can't be broken,
And these words are just a token.

Life's eternal flame

Our lives are just a guess,
We live to follow time,
We'll choose a random path,
That we will follow blind.

Not knowing what to come,
Obstacles in our way,
Predicting every second,
Planning every day.

Some may choose to bend the rules,
And cheat for what's to come,
By seeing in the future,
And changing what is done.

But waiting is our purpose,
And guessing is our game,
Decisions may well hurt us,
But that's life's eternal flame.

Connections

Wounds from the past may make us weak,
When tears form in our eyes,
Our hearts shall hold pure truth and honesty,
And shadow dishonest lies.

Our connections will keep us strong,
With who we choose to keep,
Our friends that find a place in us,
Appear in dreams with sleep.

And you who are anonymous,
Of who I choose to speak,
And of who I'll love,
Yes all of you!
Yes, all of you I'll keep.

K. Brooks

The moon

A piercing hole peers through the clouds,
A shimmer through the dark,
Her striking beauty of pure white brilliance,
That pureness lights my heart.

The clouds that crowd around her,
Just to fade her shine,
They fight to take her place,
Her essence so divine.

But she is not defeated,
And so the clouds surrender,
And when next the sun goes down,
Bring on the next contender.

The moon will keep on living,
Her beauty so defined,
Her power overwhelming,
She is so sublime.

Girl in the corner

That girl in the corner,
On her own.
That girl in the corner,
Always alone.
That girl in the corner,
Cries to sleep.
That girl in the corner,
Afraid to speak.
That girl in the corner,
The one that I see.
That girl in the corner,
She is me.

K. Brooks

My Island of paradise

The sea is calm tonight
The tide is full
The sun is setting
The air is cool.

The fresh smell of the ocean breeze
The clear scent of the salty sea.
A vision of paradise
A perfect island
Of clear blue seas
And crisp clear skyline.

I feel the white sand between my toes
The way the sound of the ocean flows
The feel of the waves that draw me in
The perfect warmth that wets my skin.

I feel that I could live right here
And all my years not shed a tear
For this will be my paradise island
Of clear blue seas
And crisp clear skyline.

Freedom

The birds fly free
High above the clouds
Soaring through the clear blue sky.
The feeling of hope enthrals my head
Learning I will soon get by.
The dream of escape still lives on
Knowing I will soon fly free.
The wish of freedom
No longer falling
Knowing that the bird will be me.

Sanctuary

Floating over my body,
Deep in silent thought,
Questioning all my options,
Losing battles I have fought.

Silence has consumed me,
Choice no longer there,
A prisoner in my sanctuary,
Pulling out my hair.

Look at me and who I am,
Of what I have become,
I am strong and I am loved,
But your heart has left you dumb.

Your mind is weak, your eyes are blind,
Of what you choose to see,
Your fear of losing yourself with age,
Should be your fear of losing me.

I am better off asleep,
Safe within my mind,
A perfect place, a place of peace,
Where no one will ever find.

You can't choose the ones you love,
Or who you choose to be,
You can choose who you pick,
But you cannot choose me.

Angel

Whenever I'm hurt you're always there,
I talk to you when no one cares,
You're on my side all the time,
To dry my tears when I cry.

You listen to every word I speak,
You make me strong when I am weak,
I tell you my secrets you won't let go,
You understand when I'm on my own.

You're a friend with a halo,
And wings made of gold,
A pure snow white gown,
And you'll never grow old.

You're as kind as a dolphin,
You have a heart that is whole,
Sent to me from heaven,
You're my angel.

Numb

I feel these shivers run through my body,
Making me cold when I am hot,
My tears run down my cheeks,
Trying not to bring up what I forgot.

I feel ill with regret,
Tired with sorrow,
The memories I'll cherish forever,
And start a new from tomorrow.

My hands feel numb,
My chest feels bare,
I cannot think straight,
I've lost the will to care.

I think of you each day that passes,
I'll try to move my heart along,
But each time I think,
The harder it gets,
I'll keep trying to move on.

I love you

I knew in life what I wanted to do,
I had it all planned,
I'd make it all true.

My work was my life,
So studying the key,
I'd collect my qualifications,
And live my life free.

But somewhere along,
My life's little quest,
My path cut short,
I'm put to the test.

My heart takes control,
Above my head,
So I'll fall in love,
And marry instead.

The best time in life,
Is when I'm only with you.
Reality collapses and,
It's just us two.

You make me complete,
Everything true,
You're one in a million and,
I love you.

Judgement

I saw you by the table,
Sweet and smartly dressed,
Your face just like an angel,
My love for you confessed.

The stories I had heard,
Filled my head with lies.
Of who you were to them,
Had slowly glazed my eyes.

I thought of you as thunder,
The one who made them weep,
Though I didn't know you,
My judgment couldn't keep.

But lies that were deceiving,
Didn't last for long,
You took the time to know me,
I knew that I'd been wrong.

Your kindness grew on me,
Your laugh had no compare,
Your warmth had entered through me,
I know I'd not been fair.

You rightly turned my thoughts,
The feelings I had grown,
For you I couldn't stop,
From what I had been shown.

So when I see your face,
I know that I have won,
The adventure in your eyes says,
We've only just begun.

This game

My head is spinning with worry,
Are rumours just a lie?
Are your lips unspoken?
Does bragging sit you high?

Tired with confusion,
It's not just you who does this,
Because every time I'm hurting,
From just a simple kiss.

I have this feeling that I can't control,
And when I'm with you it's wonderful.
You may lead me down a road,
Senses trained, my mind controlled,
You can make me feel this pain,
You know that you have won this game.

You fill me up with hope,
Your actions make me wonder,
Will we work this one together?
Or will friction cause our thunder?

When you're close to me,
You'll never let me leave,
But when you're far away,
It's like I've been deceived.

If you are wanting me,
You just have to say,
I can't read your mind,
And so I'll drift away.

K.Brooks

Can you feel my heart beat?
When you're close to me?
If you feel the electricity,
Then you'll know where I'll be.

Choices

From the moment I had met you,
I knew that we would click,
That you would see right through me,
And know what makes me tick.

You know all my faults,
You know all my cracks,
You know what's turning in my mind,
You break it down to facts.

You help me with my emotions,
Your words make sense to me,
We share the same connection,
Of what we want to see.

We'll talk in sense above our hearts,
Of what it's best to do,
But when it comes to these choices,
My choice should be you.

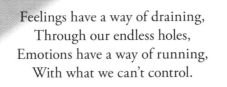

Changes

Feelings have a way of draining,
Through our endless holes,
Emotions have a way of running,
With what we can't control.

People have a way of changing,
What they say and do,
If only we could read their minds,
We'd know if they were true.

Opinions can be painful,
And lies aren't mean to scar,
Words aren't meant to hurt us,
This makes the distance far.

The walls between our thoughts,
Cuts our ties for hoping,
Our feelings seem uncertain,
Resistance slowly sloping.

Are you worth the wait?
Are you worth my time?
Should I stick around for you?
Or should I draw the line?

Complete

Dizzy from my senses,
Playing on my heart beat,
Your scent enough to calm me,
My brain accepts defeat.

Hypnotised with my memories,
A perfect calm serenity,
Fills me like a glass complete,
Changing my own entity.

The depth of any ocean,
Cannot at all compare,
To how you make me feel,
Of that I am aware.

The endless width of space,
Cannot fill my void,
But just your warm embrace,
Can hit me like an asteroid.

The endless length of time,
Counted very few,
This means nothing anymore,
Now that I've found you.

K.Brooks

I would know you blind

You are like my book of wonders,
Pages filled with gold,
You are like the fearless oceans,
Your mysteries are untold.

The beauty of your treasured soul,
Only grows on me,
How vines climb on a wall,
Or blossoms on a tree.

Never had I thought before,
That I would fall for you,
But persistence proved me wrong,
My feelings that are true.

I have learnt that in my heart
A body is a shell,
But what lies just underneath is,
A love that you can't tell.

That spark I get from your touch,
That flame within my mind,
That's what I feel when I'm with you,
And I would know you blind.

Until death do you part

In lives long and distant trek,
There's many quests we're thrown,
Like how to build a family,
That we can't do alone.

So there must come a time when,
Hearts rule out our heads,
When finally found the perfect one,
To whom you shall be wed.

You will live right by their side,
In sickness and in health,
And you may have your silly squabbles,
And trouble over wealth.

However hard your road may be,
It's nothing to compare,
Of what you will forever have,
Of the love you share.

So listen to your senses,
Be guided by your heart,
May happiness be forever more,
Until death do you part.

Lessons

When your mind goes around in circles,
Of what the past has brought,
Fighting all my losing battles,
Good lessons I've been taught.

And the past repeats itself,
The viscous circles follow me,
It's like a never ending clip,
Of what I'll always see.

So this is why I've changed my mind,
Of who I tend to choose,
That special soul with looks discounted,
Of him I'll never lose.

World of beauty

I sit by the waterfall,
Liquid droplets patter,
On the surface mirror,
Like diamonds they do scatter.

The sound of calm serenity,
Fill my drums with peace,
Takes me to a world of beauty,
My thoughts I can release.

Nature's nectar and its bark,
Overflows- my senses brim,
When the sun goes to his bed,
It makes the lights fall dim.

And when I spy the shadowed walls,
And hear the crickets' song,
And feel the garden beneath my feet,
I know this is where I belong.

Loves contract

Lots they learned,
On the path they chose,
When battles burned,
And oceans froze.

They travelled deep,
And lost their way,
It's tough to right,
The wrongs of day.

If time stood still,
And the camera snapped,
Would they see the truth?
Of loves contract.

The rules that apply,
To the fortunate few,
Must pay a price,
For their dreams to come true.

Matches are made,
On a whim of heart,
You'll learn from mistakes,
And will never part.

The song of noon

The blinding sun ignites the sky,
The clouds fall soft around him,
Peaceful noon brings distant sound,
The echo soon falls dim.

The faint rush of the glistening river,
The sun does gleam across it,
Like specks of diamonds lost at sea,
This evening scene is lit.

Playful grass dances quick,
They hear the crickets' tune,
The wind blows the reeds in time,
To the song of noon.

Frozen

Darkness outside my window,
The cold is in my core,
My temperature has dropped too low,
My heart will need to thaw.

I thought I knew you well,
I thought that you were different,
You had me fooled, I bow to you,
Your efforts were consistent.

And you froze my mind,
Amazed by your kindness,
You were not like the other ones,
Who drove me close to madness.

But despite all the tricks,
Illusions you created,
And tears still flood my face,
Still for you I waited.

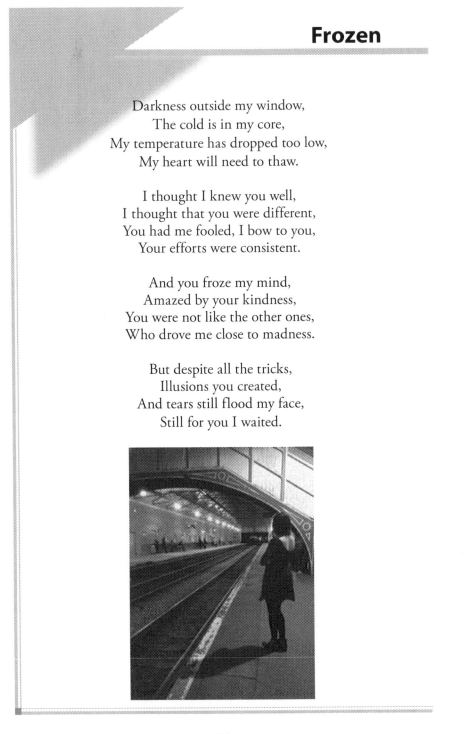

Desire and heart

You've plagued my mind a thousand times,
With the memories that surround me,
What I've felt in times that have passed,
Of what my heart knew to be.

I am trying to distinguish,
Between desire and heart,
But the two confuse me,
I can't tell them apart.

Attachment or true love?
I thought it to be the first.
But now I'm not so sure,
My feelings have me cursed!

The secret is I miss you,
Of how we used to be,
But I'll never fully understand until,
You set me free.

Gunpowder

The rose between two thorns,
Scars from battled cries,
Of wounds that cut so deep,
Where our hearts all lie.

The connections have come loose,
From where the knots were tight,
Because of realisation,
That we are just not right.

My feelings shift like earthquakes,
My tears fall like storms,
My heart a raging fire,
My thoughts will be reborn.

The walls that seal me in,
Are filled with echoed cries,
Of what plays in my head,
A tape that never dies.

On repeat, around and around,
The music getting louder,
The truth will soon explode,
Like barrels full of gunpowder.

When will I receive?
My whole heart in peace.
When can I fully rest?
When I'm not in sleep.

Gates

Should I be the chaser?
Or should I be the chased?
Where does my choice stand?
If there is only one open gate?

Do I take the risk?
Do I take the time?
When it is uncertain,
That you may not be mine.

Do the risks weigh higher?
Than uncertain gain,
For if your arrows pierce me,
Then who am I to blame?

But the riches torture,
My vixen hidden deep,
If this plays out right,
The pessimist I'll beat.

I am ready bound,
By luck that once did pass,
I thought there'd be no other,
That he would be the last.

But you I cannot shake,
From my every thought,
When, awake in deepest sleep,
A prisoner you have caught.

I cannot call the shots,
I cannot rush ahead,
Only time will tell,
What emotion will run red.

All that I can do,
Is sit around and wait,
To see how we play out,
And if you close the gate.

Let me rest

Banging on my door,
Trying to keep the peace,
But I don't want you here,
So please can you just leave?

All I asked for is time,
But you keep pushing me,
Every day I wanted,
But you won't let me be.

Let me breathe and
Give me space,
To retreat away,
To a final resting place,
Where decisions are made.

Please just let me go,
Please just let me sleep,
Don't cry your sorry cries,
Let things run as they need.

Wishing I'd not hurt you,
Wishing to forget,
That which has caused the pain,
I'm in panicked fret.

Please just let me go and
Please just let me rest,
I've tried to make this gentle,
I've tried my very best.

K.Brooks

Howling freedom

Crashing mountains beckon,
Thunder lights the sky,
Tides are raging over,
How much the passion tries.

The wolf is howling freedom,
To the moon inside,
Of what became unfrozen,
The truth could not disguise.

The battle finally over,
The tears are finally shed,
The winners choose their allies,
And leave the guilt for dead.

Now that we get closure,
Now we have the goal,
Of what joy we've been searching,
To loosen the control.

I did take the risk,
I did take the time,
When it was uncertain,
But now you can be mine.

Would you wear a ring for me?

How long do I see me and you?
As long as you want me too,
How many times will I feel your kiss?
As many times that you do wish.

Will you hold my hand in times of trouble?
Do you see me in your bubble?
Would you wear a ring for me?
For everyone else to see.

Would you catch me when I fall?
Would yours be the only name I call?
Would you walk me down the aisle?
Just seeing me would make you smile.

Would you wash my hands and feet?
When I'm old and grey and weak.
Will you love me until my death?
Would you lay me down to rest?

Would you lay flowers at my grave?
And visit me beyond our days?
When tonight I go to sleep,
Will I know if it's you I'll forever keep?

A dream, a vision

In my dreams I saw you here,
A surprise unplanned you came to me,
Just what I had pictured,
Of how your face would be.

The softness of your lips,
The taste was so divine,
I just wanted to dream on,
Feeling our bodies entwined.

When I looked into your eyes,
A future I could see,
Of passion and of love,
A vision of you and me.

I placed my hands on yours,
You took them without hesitation,
You brought them to your lips,
My gaze held, infatuation.

You held me in your embrace,
I lay my head against your chest,
Your scent was strong and oh so sweet,
You had me gently caressed.

You placed your hand behind my head,
And kissed me once again,
You stroked my cheek and found my eyes
You took away my pain.

I think that I have found my cure
To unchain the girl inside,
From her shackles you set her free,
Because you will stand by her side.

What's the point?

What's the point in living?
If you have nothing to live for.
What's the point in trying?
If you've been knocked down, too many times before.

What's the point in hoping?
If your dreams have never come true.
What's the point in caring?
If no one cares about you.

The world around me is changing,
Yet I still feel I'm stuck,
In this never-ending cycle,
Of continuous bad luck.

Time is never-ending,
The days all blur as one,
Sanity slowly slipping
My will to live is gone.

Loss of limb

It's not like we've been here before,
In ages past it was not needed,
Advancing every day we live,
Prospects for it, now exceeded.

Loss of limb can now compare to,
With metal and of wires,
If we do not have a phone,
We're thought to be retired.

Curiosity killed the cat

Did I throw it all away too soon?
Forgot what I had?
Did greed have its way with me?
The memories are so sad.

Curiosity did kill the cat,
And so it did kill me,
For I could not accept the fact,
That I wasn't to be free.

A lesson in true love,
Does not appear in haste,
But only grows with time,
This time is not a waste.

Loneliness my master

The tears that burn my cheeks,
My mind is lost to dark,
Happy only when at sleep,
Where did I go wrong?
When did this all start?

Suffocating, just taking breaths,
A sickness in my heart,
My whole body succumbed to this,
My dreams are ripped apart.

Loneliness is my master,
And I am just its slave,
It will follow me forever,
Forever to my grave.

If I was the only one

Praying that I see a light,
When the world is at war,
With natural disasters
We haven't seen before.

What if flames engulfed the trees?
The ocean drowned the land?
What if disease took control?
Who'd be left to stand?

If I was the only one,
How would I live my life?
No chance to carry on my line,
No chance to be a wife.

Would the silence overbear?
Would boredom grate away?
At the drawn-out, lonely years
That I'd take day by day.

No warmth to heat a freezing house,
No embrace to keep me sane,
No light to lead me in the dark,
No mention of my name.

What becomes of loneliness?
Of bitter truth and hate,
Of everything you once did love
But now it's just too late.

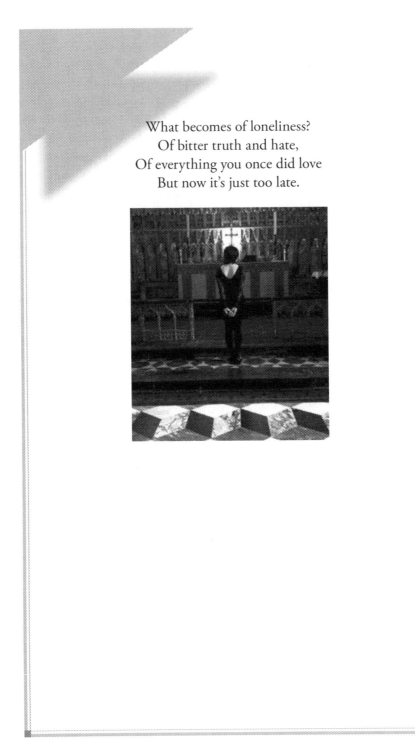

Your St. Christopher

Take my hand and I will be your guide
Through the maze of fiery hell
Follow me, break through your fear
Your soul you will not sell.

Don't let them enter your mind
Don't let them plant a seed
Don't water it or it shall grow
Don't let them see you bleed.

Let me heal your wounds,
Let me kiss your scars,
Let me venture deep inside,
I promise I'll not go far.

I will try to carry you
Over the rivers deep
Like your St. Christopher
When you are feeling weak.

I'll be the comfort to your pain,
To let you know I'm there,
I will never give up on you,
I will always care.

Fairy tale to dark

Desperate measures call for last resort,
Tried and tested and all we sought
Actions carry heavy burden
With how we keel- results uncertain
The rollercoaster looks so steep
No ups just downs, oh how I weep
Electric no longer fuels the spark
But only surges, throwing us to dark.
The flickers that fly keep doubt at bay
That hope will bail us out one day
That the rollercoaster hides a dip
To cut the nauseous nightmare clip
Will love conquer and prevail?
Will good win out this fairy tale?

Downward Spiral

Feeling like there's no way out,
The words I can't contain,
The scenes keep playing on a loop,
They always stay the same.

By no means did I feel despair,
Before you held me under,
I can't shake the feeling you didn't care,
Now you can't fix the blunder.

I cut my way through blinding dark,
Alone at first I keeled,
I'm held afloat by hope so thin,
Your transparency revealed.

Wandering along the narrow corridor,
Pictures hang on the wall,
Of the history that kills me now,
You keep letting me fall.

In the end

The war is at an end
The virus spreading fast
Weakens me internally
This illness won't just pass.

My conscience now controlled
By false hopes and dreams
That's formed in little pills,
Depression's what it seems.

Why should I accept
The hell you trapped me in,
Hear out your sorry pleas,
When you won't accept your sin?

For what I now do see,
The demons hold the earth,
All good has drained away
What is my life worth?

If I died tomorrow,
Would you even know?
Would you wish to turn back time?
And never let me go?

Now that I know

Use me, abuse me
What have you done?
Push me and shove me
Inside I'm undone.

Betray me, confuse me
I thought you were trying
To mend my lost soul
When inside I'm dying.

Waiting and waiting
For you to come home
But you keep on drifting
So that I am alone.

Deceiving, I'm screaming
For you to return
With the lessons you're given
But still you don't learn.

Cut me and scar me
Inside I am torn
Bruise me and freeze me
To the ends of my core.

Watch me and lure me,
How selfish you are!
But now that I know
You can watch me afar.

Let it burn me down

I'm getting worse
And it's far too late
To try and fix me
When I'm in this state.

You can hold my hand
You can kiss my lips
You can stroke my hair
So that I am whipped.

My temple on fire
Let it burn me down
Don't douse the fire,
Let it go to town!

If you could feel my pain
If you could understand
Just what's in my head,
And what's in my hands.

Self-centred thoughts
I let them go too far
But I am close to crazy
Do you see my scars?
I try to be your bridge
So you can see the light
But I seem to cause
These never ending fights.

So you think I lie
When I say it's you
When you are my life
All I feel is you.

You complete my heart
You've possessed my soul
You now own my body
I follow your control.

What would it take?

What would it take?
To grab a knife
What would it take?
To end this life.
What would it take?
To keep on living
When they keep taking and I keep giving.
What did it take?
To feel this way.
To learn more truths day by day.
What does it take?
To stop the wars
For oil and gas
For peace they swore.
Why do they make us learn their sin?
That the earth is dying…
That we won't win.
We're doomed to a life
Advancing machines
To political greed
Hear my silent scream!

Acknowledgments

I would like to say a massive thank you for everyone that helped put my book together, especially to my two wonderful models Samantha Moulden and Macauley Cross. The photos are wonderful and express so much emotion. Thank you for the inspiration of finally publishing my work, Kat Thornley, and thank you to everyone who has given me the inspiration to write my poems. Finally thank you to my councillor, Mel Pearson, for encouraging me to carry on writing and to Beverley Minster, who allowed me access to the Minster architecture and graveyard, making the images possible.

Poet and photographer: Kiana Brooks
Editor: Kat Thornley
Illustrator and model: Samantha Moulden
Model: Macauley Cross

Printed in the United States
By Bookmasters